William Sumner Barton

Inscriptions from the Old Burial Grounds in Worcester, Massachusetts

From 1727 to 1859. With biographical and historical notes.

William Sumner Barton

Inscriptions from the Old Burial Grounds in Worcester, Massachusetts
From 1727 to 1859. With biographical and historical notes.

ISBN/EAN: 9783337191795

Printed in Europe, USA, Canada, Australia, Japan

Cover: Foto ©ninafisch / pixelio.de

More available books at **www.hansebooks.com**

PROCEEDINGS

— OF THE —

Worcester Society of Antiquity,

FROM ITS INSTITUTION JAN. 21, 1875, TO THE
RE-ORGANIZATION UNDER THE GENERAL LAWS OF THE COMMONWEALTH,

March 6th, 1877;

TOGETHER WITH THE

CONSTITUTION AND BY-LAWS

AND

CERTIFICATE OF INCORPORATION.

WORCESTER, MASS.:
PUBLISHED BY THE SOCIETY.
1877.
U. S. A. CI.

Officers for 1877.

Members.

Samuel Elias Staples,	Worcester.
Daniel Seagrave,	Worcester.
Franklin Pierce Rice,	Worcester.
John George Smith,	Worcester.
Richard O'Flynn,	Worcester.
Rev. Albert Tyler,	Oxford.
Henry Davis Barber,	Worcester.
Henry Francis Stedman,	Worcester.
William Macready,	Worcester.
Olin Lane Merriam,	Worcester.
Herbert Henry Thompson,	Worcester.
Elijah Harrington Marshall,	Worcester.
William Augustus Sheldon,	Worcester.
William Blaine Howe,	Worcester.
Charles Renssalaer Johnson, A. B.,	Worcester.
James Andrew Smith, Esq.,	Worcester.
Augustus Stone,	Worcester.
Hon. Clark Jillson,	Worcester.
Edward Richadson Lawrence,	Worcester.
Henry Phelps,	Worcester.
Albert Alfonzo Lovell, Esq.,	Worcester.
Ellery Bicknell Crane, Esq.,	Worcester.
Augustus Coolidge,	Worcester.
Rev. Thomas Elliott St. John, A. M.,	Worcester.
Edward Issachar Comins,	Worcester.
Thomas Melvin Lamb,	Worcester.
Dwight Armsby Davis,	Worcester.
Benjamin John Dodge,	Worcester.
Isaac Newton Metcalf,	Worcester.
George Sumner,	Worcester.
Joseph Nye Bates, M. D.,	Worcester.
Alexander Cole Munroe,	Worcester.
Dr. Charles Whitney Estabrook,	Worcester.

Commonwealth of Massachusetts.

BE IT KNOWN, That whereas SAMUEL ELIAS STAPLES, CLARK JILLSON, ELLERY B. CRANE, DANIEL SEAGRAVE, FRANKLIN PIERCE RICE, JAMES ANDREW SMITH, ALBERT ALFONZO LOVELL and ALBERT TYLER, have associated themselves with the intention of forming a corporation under the name of

The Worcester Society of Antiquity,

for the purpose of cultivating and encouraging among its members a love and admiration for antiquarian research and archæological science; and, so far as practicable, to rescue from oblivion any historical matter that might otherwise be lost; also, the collection and preservation of antiquarian relics of every description, with a capital of an amount not yet established, nor divided into shares, and have complied with the provisions of the Statutes of this Commonwealth in such case made and provided, as appears from the certificate of the President, Treasurer, and Directors of said corporation duly approved by the Commissioner of Corporations, and recorded in this office :

Now, Therefore, I, HENRY B. PEIRCE, Secretary of the Commonwealth of Massachusetts, DO HEREBY CERTIFY, that said S. E. STAPLES, C. JILLSON, E. B. CRANE, D. SEAGRAVE, F. P. RICE, J. A. SMITH, A. A. LOVELL and A. TYLER, their associates and successors, are legally organized and established as and are hereby made an existing corporation, under the name of THE WORCESTER SOCIETY OF ANTIQUITY, with the powers, rights and privileges, and subject to the limitations, duties and restrictions, which by law appertain thereto.

[L. S.]   WITNESS my official signature hereunto subscribed, and the seal of the Commonwealth of Massachusetts hereunto affixed this twenty-second day of March, in the year of our Lord one thousand eight hundred and seventy-seven.

HENRY B. PEIRCE,

Secretary of the Commonwealth.

PROCEEDINGS.

PROCEEDINGS

FOR 1875.

ORIGIN OF THE SOCIETY.

The wants and needs of a community like the one in which we live, both present and prospective, are liable to remain unsatisfied unless some person volunteers to give direction to individual thought, so that each may understand the wants of the many, and all unite their efforts to promote a common cause.

The union of distinct and independent forces, the bringing together of isolated rays of intellectual light, and the aggregation of individual research, require such peculiar talent as would seem to be beyond the comprehension of a large majority of mankind.

That there has been, and now is, in the city of Worcester, a considerable number of persons, including some in the humble walks of life, who have been and are deeply interested in the preservation from oblivion of all historical matter relating to Worcester or Worcester County, as well as in the collection of rare and ancient books, pamphlets, prints, engravings. pictures, autographs and coins, together with imple-

2

ments and manufactures representing the arts, sciences and industry of former generations, no reasonable person will venture to doubt. Though their tastes were in many respects similar, they were not acquainted with each other, and, so far as their antiquarian research was concerned, each was confined to the narrow limit of the meagre result of his own efforts, without receiving any substantial benefit from what others had accomplished.

The bringing together of some of these persons for the purpose of forming a Society is due to the foresight and ability of SAMUEL E. STAPLES, who, after consultation with one or two others, sent out the following brief card of invitation :

WORCESTER, MASS., January 21st, 1875.

To John G. Smith, Daniel Seagrave, Richard O'Flynn and Franklin P. Rice:

Gentlemen—It has been proposed to form a Society for the purpose of increasing an interest in archæological science, and to rescue from oblivion such historical matter as would otherwise be lost; and you are respectfully invited to meet a few gentlemen for consultation and such action as may be thought best, at the house of the writer, No. 1 Lincoln Place (rear of No. 69 Lincoln street,) on Saturday next at 4 o'clock P. M. Hoping you may find it convenient to be present for an hour,

I am, yours respectfully,

SAMUEL E. STAPLES.

The first preliminary meeting was held January 24th, 1875, at the residence of Samuel E. Staples, No. 1 Lincoln Place, Worcester, Mass., in accordance with the above invitation. There were present, besides Mr. Staples, John G. Smith, Richard O'Flynn and

Franklin P. Rice. The matter involved in the invitation to this meeting was freely discussed, and it was the unanimous opinion of those present that an organization formed for the purposes set forth in said invitation would be useful and desirable, provided a sufficient number of persons could be found who would take an interest therein.

Mr. Staples presented the following Constitution for consideration, and the meeting was then adjourned to January 30th:

CONSTITUTION.

NAME AND PURPOSE.

ARTICLE 1. The name of this organization shall be THE WORCESTER SOCIETY OF ANTIQUITY, and its object and purpose to foster in its members a love and admiration for antiquarian research and archæological science, and the rescue from oblivion of such historical matter as would otherwise be lost.

MEMBERS.

ARTICLE 2. Any person of good character, having an interest in the objects of this Society, and having been proposed at a previous meeting, may be admitted by a majority vote of the members present, on condition of contributing to its interests, attending its meetings, and conforming to the rules and regulations of the Society.

OFFICERS.

ARTICLE 3. The officers of the Society shall consist of a President, Vice President, Secretary, Treasurer and Librarian, who shall be elected annually, in the month of January, on separate ballots, and shall respectively hold their office until a successor is chosen.

MEETINGS.

ARTICLE 4. Meetings for business and for the general good of the Society shall be held on the last Saturday of each month, excepting July and August, and as much more frequently as the interests of the Society may require; and it shall be the duty of the President and Secretary, jointly, to notify the members in writing of the time and place of all stated meetings, and of all other meetings which in their judgment the interests of the association require should be held.

QUORUM.

ARTICLE 5. Five members shall constitute a quorum for the transaction of business; but a less number may hold meetings for consultation and general improvement.

EXPENSES.

ARTICLE 6. The expenses of the Society shall be liquidated by voluntary contributions from its members, or others who may be interested in the objects of the association.

ALTERATIONS.

ARTICLE 7. This Constitution may be altered or amended in such manner as the interests of the Society may require; notice of such alteration or amendment having been given at a previous meeting, two-thirds of the members voting therefor.

The second preliminary meeting was held at the printing office of Tyler & Seagrave, No. 442 Main street, Worcester, Mass., Jan. 30th, 1875. Present, Samuel E. Staples, John G. Smith, Franklin P. Rice and Daniel Seagrave. Samuel E. Staples was chosen chairman and Daniel Seagrave secretary. On motion of Mr. Seagrave, it was unanimously voted that those present form themselves into a Society, the objects thereof to be such as set forth in the circular of invitation.

The Constitution presented at the previous meeting was read and referred to a committee consisting of Samuel E. Staples and John G. Smith.

The third preliminary meeting was held Feb. 13th, 1875, at the same place as the former meeting, and was called to order by the chairman. There were present Samuel E. Staples, John G. Smith, Franklin P. Rice, Richard O'Flynn, Henry D. Barber, Henry F. Stedman and Daniel Seagrave. The committee to whom was referred the Constitution made the following report:

WORCESTER, Feb. 13th, 1875.

The committee to whom was referred the draft of a Constitution for revision have attended to their duty, and submit the following report:

After duly considering the various names that have been suggested for the association, they have unanimously agreed that the one first proposed, viz.: "THE WORCESTER SOCIETY OF ANTIQUITY," is the most suitable, as it covers the whole ground for which the association is to be formed, and is sufficiently comprehensive to embrace all persons, in every place, who may desire to become members of the association, and the committee therefore recommend its adoption.

Article second is so changed that propositions shall be in writing, and a two-thirds vote of members present be required to admit members.

Article fourth is presented in a new draft.

Article sixth, for the word "shall" read "may," and the following additional clause: "but in case the necessity arise, the members may be assessed for such amount as the interests of the Society require."

The proposed Constitution, as revised by these and other amendments herein specified, will then read as follows:

CONSTITUTION.

NAME AND PURPOSE.

ARTICLE 1. The name of this organization shall be THE WORCESTER SOCIETY OF ANTIQUITY, and its object and purpose to foster in its members a love and admiration for antiquarian research and archaeological science, and to rescue from oblivion such historical matter as would otherwise be lost.

MEMBERS.

ARTICLE 2. Any person of good character, having an interest in the objects of this Society, and having been proposed in writing at a previous meeting, may be admitted by a two-thirds vote of the members present, on condition of contributing to its interests, attending the meetings, so far as practicable, and conforming to the rules and regulations of the Society.

OFFICERS.

ARTICLE 3. The officers of the Society shall consist of a President, Vice President, Secretary, Treasurer and Librarian, who shall be elected annually, at the stated meeting in January, on separate ballots, and shall respectively hold their office until a successor is chosen.

MEETINGS.

ARTICLE 4. Meetings for business and for the general interests of the Society shall be held on the first Tuesday of each month, excepting July and August; and also such special meetings as the interests of the Society may require; and it shall be the duty of the President and Secretary, jointly, to notify the members in writing of the time and place of all stated meetings, and of all special meetings which in their judgment (or upon the written request of any three members,) the interests of the association require should be held.

QUORUM.

ARTICLE 5. Five members shall constitute a quorum for the transaction of business, but a less number may hold meetings for consultation and general improvement.

EXPENSES.

ARTICLE 6. The expenses of the Society may be liquidated by voluntary contributions of its members, or other persons who may be interested in the objects of the association; but in case the necessity arise, the members may be assessed for such amount as the interests of the Society require.

ALTERATIONS.

ARTICLE 7. This Constitution may be altered or amended at any stated meeting of the Society, notice of such alteration or amendment having been given in writing at a previous business meeting, two-thirds of the members present voting therefor.

All of which is respectfully submitted.

SAMUEL E. STAPLES,
JOHN G. SMITH.

The above Constitution was unanimously adopted.

The first regular meeting of THE WORCESTER SOCIETY OF ANTIQUITY, under the Constitution, was held at the printing office of Tyler & Seagrave, No. 442 Main street, Worcester, Mass., March 2d, 1875. There were present Henry D. Barber, Richard O'Flynn, Franklin P. Rice, John G. Smith, William Macready and Daniel Seagrave. In the absence of the chairman, Henry D. Barber was elected chairman *pro tem.* The Society was then duly organized by the election of the following officers:

President, Samuel E. Staples; Vice President, Henry D. Barber; Secretary, Daniel Seagrave; Treasurer, Henry F. Stedman; Librarian, John G. Smith.

Thus was organized a society whose future promises the most gratifying results. A committee, consisting of John G. Smith and Daniel Seagrave, was appointed to take into consideration certain amendments to the Constitution.

The next meeting was held April 6th, 1875. The President, who was absent at the time of his election, favored the Society with the following address:

ADDRESS OF THE PRESIDENT.

THE WORCESTER SOCIETY OF ANTIQUITY is designed to encourage historical research. That there is a necessity for such an organization in this community may be seen when we consider that in this city of fifty thousand inhabitants, with its many institutions of learning (in literature, art and the sciences,) there is no other institution of this kind that meets the popular demand. The American Antiquarian Society may be properly called a national institution, supported and maintained by gentlemen of eminence in their several walks and professions, embracing in its membership persons of the rarest culture and most profound knowledge. Such an institution is useful beyond calculation, in securing, developing and preserving historical knowledge, but it fails to meet the wants of many persons interested in like researches and purposes, who are not so fortunate as to be reckoned among the members of so honorable a body.

It is hoped and believed that this new Society may meet this demand, while it will in no sense be regarded as a rival of the older Society, but rather an auxiliary to it. In order, then, for this association to be the most useful to its members, and ultimately to the public at large, it is very important that each one of us pursue with diligence and careful inquiry the several topics of interest that fall within our sphere.

Historical research and the preservation of historical matter is the underlying principle that should prompt us in our efforts for the attainment and the dissemination of knowledge. Though this Society enters the field of inquiry, the paths of which have been travelled by so many illustrious men, there is room enough and to spare for the few congenial minds with which we start our organization, and the prospective numbers, large and cultivated as we expect them to be in the future, who may be attracted to this organization. The natural benefits to be derived from this association are not to be overlooked. The field of inquiry is so broad that each one may here and there cull a flower with which to beautify our institution, or bring in the harvested fruit to enrich our membership. Let each one do his part, both in spring-time and harvest, that our garners may be filled.

By the records of the last meeting, it appears by the votes then cast you did me the honor to elect me as the first President of this Society. While I appreciate the honor thus conferred, I can only wish that it had fallen upon some other person much better qualified, or that I could bring more ability to the performance of the duties of the office. Desiring the growth and prosperity of this new organization, I shall do what I can to promote its interests, doubting not but that I shall receive the hearty coöperation of all its members.

At the regular meeting held May 4th, 1875, the Committee on Amendments to the Constitution, appointed March 2d, 1875, reported an article relating to honorary members, which was adopted and numbered three (3), the numbers of the following articles being changed to correspond therewith. This article was as follows:

HONORARY MEMBERS.

ARTICLE 3. Any person of good moral character, interested in antiquarian research, and having a desire to assist in the objects of this Society, and having been proposed in writing at a previous meeting, may be admitted an honorary member thereof on receiving a two-thirds vote of the members present. Honorary members shall be entitled to all the privileges of other members, except the right to vote and hold office.

The last meeting of the year was held December 7th, 1875, at the residence of John G. Smith, No. 53 Lincoln street. At the close of the meeting remarks were made by the members relating to the prosperity of the Society during its brief existence. Mr. John G. Smith said that he felt very much encouraged by the present condition of the Society; that it had far exceeded his utmost expectations; and he congratulated the members on the benefit they had already derived from their connection with it. At the close of this year the Society was composed of twelve members.

3

The interest manifested on the part of the friends of this Society, in its progress and welfare, cannot fail to produce the most satisfactory results. The large number of books, many of them rare and expensive, collected by the members of this Society during the present year, will have a tendency to stimulate more persistent efforts in the same direction during the year to come. Our members now have in their libraries some of the oldest and rarest printed books in existence; and when these collections are brought together they will form one of the most valuable antique libraries in the country.

With these encouragements the Society closes the first year of its existence; and the members feel that they are justified in expressing their complete confidence in the success of this new enterprise.

PROCEEDINGS

For the Year 1876.

————————•◦•————————

The first annual meeting of THE WORCESTER SOCIETY OF ANTIQUITY was held at the residence of Samuel E. Staples, President of the Society, at No. 1 Lincoln Place, Worcester, Mass., January 4th, 1876. At this meeting the following officers were elected:

President, Samuel E. Staples; Vice President, Henry D. Barber; Secretary, Daniel Seagrave; Treasurer, Henry F. Stedman; Librarian, John G. Smith.

The President delivered his address, as follows:

Gentlemen—In accepting the position to which by your votes I have been assigned for another year, I desire to return my sincere thanks for the confidence shown and the honor conferred upon me.

Conscious in some measure of the poor qualifications I bring to the performance of the duties of the office, yet with the aid and coöperation that I hope to receive at the hands of every member, I trust and sincerely hope that we shall be able to place this Society upon a sure foundation, and make it an organization the power and usefulness of which shall be acknowledged wherever it may be known.

With gratitude to that Being without whose notice not a sparrow falls to the ground, let us be mindful of His goodness and mercy to us in the past, and let us strive faithfully in the future to perform with diligence the obligation of each passing hour.

And now as we enter upon the duties of a new year, this Society observes its first anniversary. Thus far of short duration, little experience and few in numbers, some of whom have been classed as " *middle men*," * nevertheless the purposes of the organization have been accomplished in the encouragement of historical research and the preservation of historical matter. Associated labor is calculated to produce much greater results than the independent effort of an individual alone. By association we are quickened and incited to greater diligence and stronger effort, consequently more is accomplished than could be done without such united purpose. The advantages of associations like our own are apparent, and no argument is needed to show their importance.

The recent circular from the commissioners of the proposed centennial celebration, recommending that an historical address, having special reference to local history, be delivered in every town or county throughout the land on the coming anniversary of American Independence, and that such productions be preserved and bound together by States, forming a grand history of our country, is a judicious and wise suggestion, and should have the hearty support of every patriot and every historical society throughout our vast domain.

Since the institution of THE WORCESTER SOCIETY OF ANTIQUITY, Jan. 24th, 1875, twelve meetings have been held, including three preliminary meetings. These have been occasions of considerable interest to those who have been present, and not without beneficial results. Matters relating to the association have been discussed, new members have been admitted from time to time, and reports of the acquisitions have been made, showing in the aggregate not less than 1000 volumes and 1500 pamphlets,†besides numerous portraits, autographs and coins.

One pleasant feature of our association has been in holding the meetings of the Society at the dwellings of the members, thus affording an opportunity for a better acquaintanceship of the members and the examination of their libraries, by which we have been

* Vide Proceedings American Antiquarian Society, Oct. 21, 1874.
†So far as reported, 1812 volumes and 1586 pamphlets.

instructed and entertained, and some exchanges have been effected to mutual advantage.

It would doubtless have been an easy matter to greatly increase our membership, but our purpose has been to admit only those who are especially interested in the objects of the association, and who will add to its interests by hearty coöperation in our endeavors to promote its usefulness. Numbers do not constitute true strength; this only results from earnest, active effort on the part of those who are associated together for a common purpose.

Having thus far reviewed the brief history of our Society, let us now inquire what it shall be in the future. Shall it go on increasing in usefulness and multiplying its numbers, or shall it be suffered to languish and die, failing to meet the demands of the place and the times? I think you will agree with me in saying it ought to and must be sustained.

I venture to affirm that not one who has helped the Society through its first year of existence would be willing to see it fall to the ground as unripe fruit, unfit for a place among the honored societies of the land, having a kindred purpose in their life and continuance with our own.

This Society is not alone in laboring under embarrassments in the early stages of its existence; and we should not therefore be discouraged, for a brighter day is sure to dawn if we prove faithful to the trust now imposed upon us.

We should receive a new impetus from the inspiration of this centennial year, and strive with renewed diligence and energy to do our part in treasuring up the records of the past and being prepared to transmit to posterity that which we have obtained.

In the language of another, "our first and great object is to rescue from the past all that is valuable in regard to New England (and I will add our whole country), and to preserve all that may in any way contribute to the history and renown of her people."

To rescue from the past—that is one of the fundamental principles of this Society. O that we knew more of the past—more concerning those noble men, the fathers of our republic, who a hundred years ago were striving and toiling here to establish a government that should bless and elevate mankind and make them free.

While we cannot know all we desire, yet history reveals unto us enough to kindle anew our patriotism and lead us to a greater, a deeper and truer devotion to the interests of our common country. To rescue from the past—that shall be our motto. Let nothing worthy of preservation be lost, but gather up the threads of history, weave them together, and let them be preserved through all coming time.

But why so anxious about the past? Is it not the future that most concerns us? Most truly it is; but only as we rightly know and estimate the past shall we learn wisdom for the future. The noble, patriotic and Christian example of our worthy sires shall be a pattern for us, in so far as they were exemplars of all that is good and true in man, and we will strive to imitate their virtues and avoid their errors.

Having thus briefly considered the interests, purposes and design of this association, let us as we now start anew in life's pilgrimage, ever strive faithfully to perform our part of its duties, so that the world around us may be better for the work we may have done.

At this meeting the matter of printing the proceedings of the Society was referred to a committee consisting of Daniel Seagrave, Richard O'Flynn and Franklin P. Rice, who reported at the next meeting in favor of printing the proceedings, but final action was deferred till March 7th, 1876, when the subject was indefinitely postponed, and a committee consisting of Daniel Seagrave, Henry D. Barber and James A. Smith was appointed to take into consideration the expediency of printing the Constitution and By-Laws. After investigating the matter, it was thought expedient to revise the Constitution, and at the regular meeting held October 3d, 1876, a committee consisting of Samuel E. Staples, Daniel Seagrave and Ellery B. Crane was appointed to make such revision;

and at the meeting held November 11th the committee was enlarged by adding to its number Clark Jillson and James A. Smith.

This committee held several meetings, and at the last meeting of the year, held December 5th, 1876, at the residence of John G. Smith, 53 Lincoln street, the committee reported a revised Constitution, which was considered, approved and laid over till the next meeting for final adoption.

At the meeting held May 2d, 1876, a committee consisting of Franklin P. Rice, Richard O'Flynn and Augustus Stone was appointed to draw up and forward resolutions to Henry B. Anthony, Senator in Congress from Rhode Island, thanking him, in the name of the Society, for securing the passage of a bill in Congress having for its object the placing of the public documents within the reach of the people; and at the meeting of June 6th the committee reported the following resolution:

Resolved, That the thanks of this Society be tendered to the Hon. He. 'y B. Anthony for the introduction of the bill providing for the sale and better distribution of the Public Documents.

Resolved, That this resolution be entered upon the records of the Society, and that a copy be forwarded to Senator Anthony.

The Secretary was instructed to forward the above, and received the following reply:

PROVIDENCE, May 17, 1876.

DEAR SIR—Your note of the 12th was forwarded to me from Washington. Please express to the Society my thanks for the complimentary resolution of which you apprise me.

Yours, very respectfully,

H. B. ANTHONY.

DANIEL SEAGRAVE, Esq., Secretary.

At the same meeting, Charles R. Johnson read an interesting paper on the " Vestiges of Ancient American Civilization," as follows :

Gentlemen of The Worcester Society of Antiquity—I would invite your attention a short time this evening to the subject of American archæology. The study of the antiquities of any nation, to whatever period of time or to whatever part of the world that nation belongs, is always an entertaining one ; but the investigation becomes doubly interesting when it relates to our own ancestors, or to the remains of other races which once flourished where we now dwell. Hence we should all have a special concern in the topic before us.

In considering the ancient civilization of America, I shall confine myself to the localities where the remains are most extensive, viz.: Mexico, including Yucatan, Central America and Peru ; and I shall devote my time to the discussion of three questions : First, How high a degree of civilization is indicated? Secondly, How far back does that civilization date? and, thirdly, Who were its authors?

Beginning, then, with the first question, it should be said at the outset that very different grades of skill are to be noticed in different places. The best specimens of workmanship are seen in Yucatan and Central America. Proceeding northward, the ruins decrease in importance. Travelling to the south, one has to go as far as Ecuador before making valuable discoveries, but neither there nor in Peru are the remains equal to those of Guatemala or Yucatan. You have all heard of the ruined cities of America ; most of you have probably read the graphic accounts of them given by Stephens and Squier, hence it would be very much out of place for me here to rehearse what those eminent authors have said ; but I will briefly describe a few of the important works of the ancient people, in order that we may get some idea of their skill and draw an inference as to their condition.

At Palenque, in the Mexican State of Chiapa, there are some remarkable ruins. The most noticeable of these is a building called the " Palace." It is situated on a terraced pyramid, forty feet high. This building is 228 feet long, 180 feet wide, and 25 feet high. It has 14 doorways on each side and 11 at each end. It was built of hewn stone, carefully laid in mortar. Around the edifice was a corridor 9 feet wide, roofed by a pointed arch. There are four interior courts, one of which measures 70 by 80 feet. These courts are surrounded by corridors, the architectural work of which is richly decorated. The piers around the courts are "covered with figures in stucco, or plaster, which, when broken, reveals six or more coats or layers, each revealing traces of painting." The sculptures are very finely executed. Another edifice at Palenque, called La Cruz, is so wonderfully ornamented that Captain Dupaix declares : " It is impossible to describe adequately the interior decorations of this sumptuous temple ;" and speaking of its broken statues, Stephens says : " In justness of proportion and symmetry they must have approached the Greek models." Captain Richard Stewart, a recent traveller in Mexico, describes some wonderful ruins which he saw near Multipee, in the State of Guadalajara. These ruins are situated on a high plateau, and extend over a space of more than twenty-five acres. The most prominent among the remains is a quadrilateral pyramid 500 feet square and 100 feet in height. On the side of the pyramid facing the east is an arched doorway 39 feet high and 27 feet in width, flanked by immense sphinxes standing on marble pedestals. There are two marble pillars 45 feet high in front of each sphinx. These pillars are ornamented with finely-carved figures and are covered with hieroglyphics. Passing the grand entrance, one comes upon a stately hall, 53 by 90 feet, the walls of which are adorned with sculptured figures and hieroglyphics. The ceiling is supported by twelve marble pillars, six on each side, which are also covered with carvings. Four doors lead from this hall into smaller rooms, which it is supposed, from the character of the interior, were used as resting places of the dead. There are also doorways which lead from the main hall to flights of stone steps descending to subterranean chambers.

. In the State of Oaxaca a monument has been found which undoubtedly was once used as an astronomical observatory. This is a granite rock hewed into the shape of a pyramid, at the top of which is a level space, whence a fine view of the heavens can be had. On one side of the rock are carved astronomical figures, and

I

among these is the form of a man gazing at the sky through a telescope. There is strong evidence among the ruins that the ancient people did not neglect athletic exercises. A good example of this is shown in the Gymnasium or Tennis Court at Chicken Itza, in Yucatan, a structure formed by two parallel walls 274 feet long, 30 feet thick and 120 feet apart. In the middle of these walls, and opposite each other, are two stone rings 4 feet in diameter, and having at the centre an aperture 19 inches in diameter. These rings are 20 feet from the ground. The space between these walls was beyond question used for games, but what kind of games we cannot tell.

Thus far I have spoken only of the remains in North America, but those in South America are also very important. The city of Cuzco was defended by immense stone fortresses, the walls of which were so massive as to make it appear incredible to the conquerors that they could have been raised by human hands. The Temple of the Sun at Cuzco was a structure of extraordinary size and magnificence, having "a circuit of more than four hundred paces." A section of its walls still exist, forming a part of the Convent of St. Domingo. At Tiahuanaco there evidently once existed a great city. Cieça de Leon, describing this place, says: "There are stones so large and so overgrown that our wonder is incited, it being incomprehensible how the power of man could have placed them where we see them. They are variously wrought, and some having the form of men must have been idols. Near the walls are many caves and excavations under the earth, but in another place further west are other and greater monuments, such as large gateways with hinges, platforms and porches, each made of a single stone. It surprised me to see these enormous gateways, made of great masses of stone, some of which were thirty feet long, fifteen feet high and six thick." The great roads of Peru may, however, be regarded as the greatest monuments of the old race. One of them extended from Quito to Chili; another led from Cuzco to the coast. They were from twenty to twenty-five feet wide, and were built on a foundation of masonry. In some places they were paved, in others macadamized. Mr. Baldwin, in speaking of these roads, observes that "the builders of our Pacific Railroad, with their superior engineering skill and mechanical appliances, might reasonably shrink from the cost and the difficulties of such a work as this. Extending from one degree north of Quito to Cuzco, and from Cuzco to Chili, it was quite as long as the two Pacific railroads, and its wild route among the mountains was far more difficult." Is any further proof needed that a people who could undertake and complete works like this, and the others I have alluded to, were in a very advanced state of civilization?

I now come to the second question, How far back does this civilization date? Those who follow the generally received chronology are inclined to speak of the American ruins as of no very great age. They would make it appear that this continent, nay, that the world itself, has been peopled but a few thousand years, and that all civilization must have grown up in that time. The researches of scholars among the antiquities of Egypt, Assyria and India, as well as the discoveries of science, have established the falsity of this notion as to the Eastern Hemisphere, and I think that it may be shown to be equally untrue in regard to the Western Hemisphere. Great cities are not built in a day. Progress in science and art is of slow growth, and it is only by gradual stages that a people is raised from savagery to a state of refinement. Yucatan, Chiapa and Guatemala were covered by a dense forest when Cortez conquered Mexico, and this forest then had every appearance of having stood there for centuries. It is here that are found the most striking remains of the lost race. Here are Copan, Mitla and Palenque, or rather here are the shattered remnants of their former grandeur. If the rise of civilization is gradual, so also is its decay. How many centuries, then, must have elapsed since these cities were in their prime! How many more since the date of their foundation! Nay, further, to what remote time shall we assign the foundation of the cities which preceded these, and of whose existence there is the strongest evidence? For, as Brasseur de Bourbourg says. "among the edifices forgotten by time in the forests of Mexico and Central America, we find architectural characteristics so different from each other that it is as impossible to attribute them all to the same people as to believe they were all built at the same epoch." The condition of the remains themselves bears positive testimony to their great age.

Nothing is left but what is least destructible. Even the massive
stone buildings themselves have mostly crumbled away, and only
a few remain to attest the glory of their founders. Every wooden
structure, every tool, every article of furniture, every household
utensil, except something earthen or stone, has disappeared. The
period of time required for such a process of obliteration must be
very extended indeed. All civilized peoples have a literature
which, while it exists, gives a full account of their history. The
ancient Americans *had* a literature, but unhappily it was almost
entirely destroyed by monkish bigotry. From the little that remains we are enabled to gain a few facts regarding the history of
its authors. It appears that here, as in the Old World, one nation
succeeded another in influence and power, only to be in its turn
supplanted by a third, and thus in regular order. The prominent
people mentioned in this succession are the Chichemecs, the Colhuas, the Toltecs and the Aztecs. Under the head of Chichemecs
seem to be included all the original barbarous inhabitants of the
country. They were followed by the Colhuas, who were the
founders of the original civilization. The Toltecs came into the
country about ten centuries before the Christian era, and established themselves in the place of the Colhuas. The oldest certain
date in the Toltec history is 955 B. C. This was when the conquerors made a division of the land; whence the inference that
they began to arrive about 1000 B. C. The Toltecs had a long
lease of power, but eventually, weakened by misgovernment and
broken up by dissensions, they were forced to give place to the
Aztecs, who appeared on the scene about two hundred and fifty
years before the Spanish invasion, and continued to rule the country till they were subdued by Cortez. Thus much for the history,
as recorded in the American annals. It is but just to say that
this account seems to be in some respects corroborated by the
Phœnician and Tyrian writers, especially in regard to the antiquity
and civilization of the American races; for they record instances
of ships being driven across the Atlantic and finding a land " wat-
ered by several navigable streams and beautified with many gardens of pleasure, planted with divers sorts of trees and an abun-
dance of orchards. The towns are adorned with stately buildings
and banquetting houses, pleasantly situated in their gardens and
orchards." The time when these ships were driven across could

hardly have been later than 700 B. C., and was probably considerably earlier. I think I have shown that the civilization in North America is of a very ancient date. By a parity of reasoning, this may be proved in regard to South America. There, too, the old structures have nearly all perished, time having brought everything possible to ruin. There, again, may be collected fragments of early history, which, when put together, go to show that the country was inhabited by an intelligent race as early as 2500 B. C.

Science also lends its aid to assist in solving the question of antiquity; but as usual, when science interferes in such matters, we are carried back an almost indefinite distance. Professor Orton, in his work on "The Andes and the Amazon," makes the following remarkable declaration: "Geology and archæology are combining to prove that Sorato and Chimborazo have looked down upon a civilization far more ancient than that of the Incas, and perhaps coeval with the flint flakes of Cornwall and the shell-mounds of Denmark. On the shores of Lake Titicaca are extensive ruins which antedate the advent of Manco-Capac, and may be as venerable as the lake dwellings of Geneva. Wilson has traced six terraces in going up from the sea through the province of Esmeraldas toward Quito, and underneath the living forest, which is older than the Spanish invasion, many gold, copper and stone vestiges of a lost population were found. In all cases these relics are found below high tide mark, in a bed of marine sediment, from which he infers that this part of the country formerly stood higher above the sea. If this be true, vast must be the antiquity of these remains, for the upheaval and subsidence of the coast is exceedingly slow." I can but think that this estimation puts the origin of civilization far enough back to satisfy the most enthusiastic student of American archæology.

The third and last question, Who were the authors of this civilization? next demands our attention. This is a subject about which there has long been much dispute. Able scholars have discussed the matter with a great display of learning, and self-supposed scholars have often made it the occasion of a great display of ignorance. All sorts of theories have been advanced. Tall folios have been written to show that the American races are descended from the "lost tribes of Israel," as witness Lord Kingsborough's works. Other volumes have been prepared with a view

to establish the fact that the Phœnicians settled this continent.
Still other books attribute this work to the Malays. Mr. C. G.
Leland, an Englishman, recently made a very labored effort to
prove that ancient America was indebted to the Chinese for its
civilization, and, in strange contrast to this, Mr. Charles W. Brooks,
an American, last year read a paper before the San Francisco
Academy of Sciences, in which he attempted to show that the
Chinese race derived its origin from the Peruvians. These theories are all built upon very slender foundations, if foundation they
may be said to have at all. A stray word here, an obscure custom
there, and an odd instrument somewhere else are, in most cases,
all they have to depend upon. What if the Phœnicians and Malays *did* have communication with this continent in prehistoric
times? Does it necessarily follow from that that they peopled it
or gave it its civilization? England and France, separated only
by a narrow channel, have had constant communication with each
other for a thousand years, the respective races of each remaining
the same, and yet the English have not anglicized France, nor
have the French gallicized England. How small, then, must have
been the effect upon the character and condition of the people of
two continents, thousands of miles apart, of the scanty intercourse
brought about by the occasional visits of trading ships! As to the
"lost tribes of Israel," there is not the slightest historical evidence
that they ever left Asia, nor has anything worthy the name of
proof been discovered in this country to indicate that they were
ever here. Besides, as Mr. Baldwin justly remarks, "such a jour-
ney" as that required to bring them here, "had it been possible,
would have resulted in utter barbarism rather than any notable
phase of civilized life." If we thus reject all the old theories, it
may well be asked how we account for the presence of man on
this continent, and to whom we ascribe the construction of the
great works before mentioned. To this I answer that, for myself,
I am inclined to adopt the "Atlantic Theory," which is based on
the supposition that there formerly existed an extension of the
American continent reaching out toward the east from what is now
the Gulf of Mexico, and almost meeting Europe; that upon this
peninsula or continent there existed in prehistoric times a very
cultured people; that it was, in fact, the cradle of the civilization
of the world; that thence men went out to subdue and civilize the

rest of the earth; that by a tremendous cataclysm this land was engulfed, disappearing beneath the sea; that a few of the people escaped, and were the originators of the civilization of Mexico, Central America and Peru; that portions of the submerged territory afterward rose, forming the islands known as the Antilles. Brasseur de Bourbourg is the great exponent of this theory. This learned Frenchman spent many years in Mexico and Central America, studying among the ruins. He became master of the Maya language, and succeeded in translating the old books and in deciphering some of the inscriptions. He found abundant references to the cataclysm in the ancient manuscripts which he discovered and in the sculptures everywhere visible in the deserted cities. What is stranger still, he asserts that many of the rites practiced by the natives to-day, and which he personally observed, have special reference to the great convulsion. The common people do not know the meaning of these rites, but the priests keep the secret. Brasseur also cites several of the old Greek authors to show that the nations of the Eastern continent in ancient times had dealings with Atlantis.

I would have liked much to have discussed this theory at length, thus giving a juster account of it, but it is not possible to do so in the brief space allotted to this essay. Indeed, to treat of the subject worthily would require the whole of a separate paper, and therefore I will not attempt a further review of it here.

It has been my endeavor to show in these pages that the remains found in various parts of the continent attest that there once lived here a race of men far advanced in the arts of civilized life; that that race can be traced back to a very distant epoch; and that its origin is not to be ascribed to any of the sources which it has been the custom of most writers on this subject to point out. I am deeply sensible that these questions have been treated of very inadequately in this essay, but I trust that the lack of skill shown here will be the means of inciting other and abler investigators to research in this direction.

In closing, I desire to express my obligation to Hon. John D. Baldwin, whose work on "Ancient America" has greatly assisted in the preparation of this paper.

At a special meeting held June 9th, 1876, the Society voted not to accept the invitation to join in the public procession at the Centennial celebration on the Fourth of July, as many of its members were already engaged for duty on that day.

At the regular meeting held Sept. 12th, 1876, the following paper on "Genealogy" was read by Ellery B. Crane:

Mr. President, and Members of The Worcester Society of Antiquity —Genealogy, the history of the descent of a person or family from an ancestor, is to me a subject of particular interest; and out of my limited study of family histories has grown a desire to know something of the records of the past concerning the different races who have inhabited the earth, and particularly that ancient and unknown people who have left behind them on this American continent (as Mr. Baldwin tells us) "such lasting monuments of a certain degree of civilization." The very able and interesting essay read by Mr. C. R. Johnson at our meeting held on the evening of June 6th of the present year gave us much information concerning this ancient race; yet it left us, as no doubt it left him, thirsting after more knowledge relating to that antique people.

This same mental thirst for additional facts, either in the direction of the history of races or of families, stimulated now and then by a fresh, invigorating draught of information brought to light through the exploration of some old musty, time-worn town or church record, or it may be from the writings of some ancient English, French or Spanish traveller, or perchance it may be from a personal examination of the old ruins themselves, is perhaps one cause of the interest taken in ancient history, whether of men or nations. Yet from the remotest ages there has always existed among civilized people (and to some extent among the uncivilized) a desire to trace one's lineage and perpetuate its knowledge; it seems, therefore, a principle of our nature. One of our prominent genealogists has said that among all the motives which operate on the human mind few exert more influence than those drawn from history. If the intellectual, social and moral condition of nations rich in historical recollections be compared with that of a people chiefly or wholly destitute of them, the difference will be found to be vast and striking. The strength of England and the United States is fed continually by memories of Cressy and Agincourt, of Bunker Hill and Saratoga, while long centuries of darkness and bondage have enfeebled the Chinese and the Irish. What is true of nations is also true of families. There is scarcely to be found an intelligent, public-spirited, virtuous man who can safely deny that his motives to virtue and patriotism are not strongly reinforced by the consideration (if such were the fact) that his ancestors were brave and upright men. With Webster, let us believe that there is a moral and philosophical respect for one's ancestors which elevates the character and improves the heart. Burke truly said, " Those only deserve to be remembered by posterity who treasure up the history of their ancestors."

Our American ancestry is certainly rich in moral strength. What we are to-day depends, to a very great extent, upon what our ancestors were before us. We are moulded largely after them. Let no man place dishonor on his ancestry, but rather let it be his solemn duty to *ever* hold it in high regard. How grand the accomplishment for a person to be able to consider what his forefathers were; what they did one, two or three hundred years ago; what part they took in matters of Church or State—for there is no family without its ideal man. The history of a *nation* is largely made up of incidents of heroism or patriotism performed by its people, and really it is no more nor less than a collective history of the families composing that nation. Thus we see that by the writing of family memorials we are able to perpetuate the nation's history, and at the same time connect those families with the great transactions of the past, enabling posterity to detect what their ancestors had to do with the successive portions of the nation's life.

The publication of these pedigrees, and the holding of family meetings, or reunions as they are sometimes called, has a salutary effect; it tends to bring members of the family together and to bind them more closely in bonds of fraternal love and esteem. I have been a witness to good results from these family gatherings, and have taken great pleasure in bringing face to face relatives who might never have seen each other had it not been for the family reunion, and doubtless would never have known of each other if the family history had not been written. I have met persons who came hundreds of miles to attend a meeting of this kind, hoping that there perhaps they might be able to see, or at least gain some knowledge concerning a relative whose whereabouts for years had been unknown to them, and in almost every instance success crowned their effort.

All persons that have given much attention to family histories have become deeply impressed with the varied relationships running through the different families—how they are, as it were, woven together by marriage, one family with another. The effect is really peculiar. The descendants of families who were neighbors and intimate friends two hundred years ago find themselves to-day husband and wife. The rapidity with which they multiply seems almost incredible. In two hundred years, from one progenitor, the Rawson family increased to over seven thousand persons, including the intermarriages.

To many persons genealogy is an uninteresting subject, and slow to attract their attention; but, nevertheless, it has its ardent supporters, and not a few persons are to be found laboring studiously within this branch of historical record. They are doing a splendid work for posterity, who, in the coming ages, will rise up and call them blessed. My little experience has proven that the middle-aged persons and those past the prime of life are the most ready to take interest and render assistance in this kind of work. The younger people have so much to turn their minds in other channels, that not until they have taken upon themselves the more serious part of life and mastered many of its weighty problems, so that they begin to realize what this life means, that we should not live for mere self—then there comes the interest to be felt in others, and genealogical subjects are more readily taken up. Educated, thoughtful, representative men are always found ready to give their attention to this theme, so far as circumstances will admit. A man must, indeed, entertain a very low estimate for ancestral worth, and show very little regard for those noble patriarchs who spent their lives in improving and perfecting the institutions which are to be so much enjoyed by every successive generation, if he is not willing, either with his time or money, to encourage the publication of family pedigrees, and the influence arising from such unwillingness cannot work for good upon the minds of *his children* or those that come after them.

Among the first questions that press themselves upon the mind of the genealogist for solution, these are perhaps the most prominent: Who were our first progenitors? From whence did they come? When did they arrive in this country? What was their condition in the old country? When, where and how did they live? What were their occupations? What their characteristics, physical, moral? What position in society did they sustain? What (if any) were the principal incidents of their lives? These and many more must arise. But how and where can the answers be obtained? Those who have had the most experience are the best prepared to point out the way of solution. I do not claim to have had sufficient practical acquaintance with the subject to be able to dictate largely to others, but perhaps I can, in a general way, make some suggestions and give some hints that will prove of service to those of you who may enter upon this interesting yet mysterious, and sometimes almost fruitless, voyage.

The answer to the first question, Who was our first progenitor? and perhaps to some of the others that follow, may be found in tradition. Many persons are able to tell you they are descended from Baronet or Sir Knight So-and-So, General Brown or Capt. Smith, who, years gone by, served his country with distinction and renown; but about anything intermediate between that period and the record of their own family, they know nothing and care little. But this man, so proud of his nobility as to cherish and pass down to his children the name of their progenitor, renders valuable service in furnishing the family genealogist with the key-note to a melody which may gladden the hearts of thousands of their fellow kin. After personal inquiries among the eldest surviving members of the family, should tradition fail to furnish the coveted solution, then search for the family records, and trace them back to the fountain-head. "Hotten's List of Emigrants to America" may perhaps give the name and time of arrival in this country. This book of Hotten's gives the names of a large number of persons who went from Great Britain to the American plantations from the year 1600 to 1700, with their ages, locations, where they formerly lived in the mother country, and names of the ships in which they embarked, taken from manuscript records preserved in the Public Records Office, London, by John C. Hotten, and published in 1874.

It is very difficult to obtain satisfactory accounts of their condition in the mother country, and also where and how they lived, without visiting the old localities and examining the records that may be found there.

Histories of nearly if not all the counties in England have been published, some of them, I am told, entering largely into family pedigrees, and they are very much needed by American genealogists, in order that the connecting links between the old English stock and the early settlers of the New England colonies may be better adjusted and understood. At the present time very few of these county histories are to be found in the United States. But Congress has taken the matter in hand, and an order has been passed to have them purchased for our National Library, where they may be consulted. Indexes to some of these histories are to be found in some American libraries, but they are by no means common. I anticipate that the wants of many persons who are anxious to find records of their ancestry in England will be gratified when a complete set of English county histories shall have become the property and in the possession of a public library on this side of the water.

There are some standard books for genealogical reference to be found at the Antiquarian Library of our city, such as the New England Historical and Genealogical Register, numbering some thirty volumes; Dr. Savage's Genealogical Dictionary; Henry Bond's family memorials and genealogies of the families and descendants of the early settlers of Watertown, Mass.; Genealogical Notes, by Goodwin; Genealogical Register of the First Settlers of New England, by John Farmer; Vinton Memorials, by John A. Vinton; Littell's First Settlers of the Passaic Valley; also a very long list of county and town histories. The public owe a debt for the use of the library of the American Antiquarian Society that they never can well repay. There are by actual count 200 county and town histories containing genealogical notices of the early settlers, some of them quite extended, and many, if not the greater part of them, can be found in our Antiquarian Library.

Daniel S. Durrie, Librarian of the State Historical Society of Wisconsin, has published an alphabetic index to American genealogies and pedigrees. You will find in this index, under the name sought for, a reference given to numerous histories and works of other kinds, where perhaps the desired information may be found. There also has been prepared a catalogue of family histories by William H. Whittemore. The first edition appeared in 1862, under the title, " Handbook of American Genealogy;" the second in 1868, under the present title, "American Genealogist," which was again republished in 1875. From this catalogue reference can be had to all the American family genealogies that had been published up to the month of June, 1875.

In addition to the works already mentioned for reference, there are the numerous family histories, of which a large number can be examined at this Antiquarian Library. When unable to satisfy your desire from these family, town and county histories, then the original manuscript records of towns and church societies, where any member or your family has been a resident, must be carefully examined for births, deaths, marriages, etc. It is well to look over the probate records and registry of deeds to see what can be found there; also the inscriptions on head-stones in our old burial grounds. If all the records upon the ancient tomb-stones, marking the final resting places of our forefathers, could be transcribed before they are forever lost, it would save to posterity a valuable register, and the pen of the future genealogist would render homage to the transcriber. Already many of those pristine monuments that were standing over the dust of those once noble sires have become weakened by the decay of ages, and wherever the slab is found on the sacred spot the characters have become so obliterated by the collection of lichen and rust as to place them almost beyond recognition. A few records of this kind can be found in the Historical and Genealogical Register, but it is a source of much regret that more of them have not been preserved.

In searching records made in the early days of our colonial settlements, a peculiarity about the dates may be noticed. Our Puritan forefathers began their year with March for the first month, and the succeeding months were represented by successive numbers. This was called the Old Style legal year in England, and in use previous to the year 1752.

At the present time the town and city records of births, deaths and marriages are kept with such systematic thoroughness throughout New England, and particularly in the State of Massachusetts, that the future collector of family pedigrees will have comparatively an easy task from the present time forward, so long as the same system of registration shall be continued.

The practice adopted by many of our colleges, of keeping a record of the lives of their sons and perpetuating the prominent points in their history, will exert a good influence over them, and, in the future, prove a very valuable reference for the family genealogist.

To obtain records of a more recent date, it will be necessary, so far as possible, to have the names and the post-office address of all persons bearing the same patronymic, to gain which it will be found profitable to consult all the town, city, county and State directories, reference books of the mercantile agencies, and all other books that you can find access to, out of which you would be quite sure of acquiring a good list. In the meantime circulars could be printed, with blank spaces, to send to each person on your list, that they may fill out the blanks and return them; and it is very important that these circulars be so formed that the manner of filling up the blanks will be readily understood by those to whom they are sent, and when properly filled the information will be complete and comprehensive. Caution should be given against writing obscurely, for it sometimes happens that records not clearly written in the original manuscript cause serious errors in the printed page, impairing its value and producing dissatisfaction in the family where the inaccuracy occurs.

A work of this kind requires much time for preparation. It never should be hurried through. Success depends on its thoroughness and accuracy. Discouragements in various forms will present themselves, but with a firm determination to conquer any obstacle that stands in your way, success will at last be the reward for your labor.

Genealogical subjects did not occupy the minds of the early settlers of our New England colonies to any great extent. They were more thoughtful for the safety and welfare of their families, the enjoyment of their religious liberty, and the success of their settlements, than the publication of independent family histories. They rather preferred making their record in one grand colonial history, where each family might be represented by their self-sacrifice and devotion of life for liberty and true patriotism.

The earliest genealogy, in a distinct form, published in the United States is believed to be that of Mr. Samuel Stebbins and Hannah, his wife, from the year 1707 to the time of its publication in Hartford, Ct., in 1771, containing 24 pages, and printed by Ebenezer Watson. But one other (that of the Chauncey family, in 1787,) was published previous to 1806. From 1806 to the year 1850, 44 years, about 79 were published; within the next 10 years 63 genealogies were printed; and in the 10 years succeeding 1870, 242 came from the printer's hands; during the five years previous to 1875 (at which time my record ceases) 135 were issued, showing that there has been steadily developed a growing interest in this kind of work; and I anticipate that the number of genealogical publications for the five years ending in 1880 will far outrank that of the same period of five years preceding it.

As to the arrangement of matter for publication, style to be adopted, etc., there are almost as many different modes as there are books, for each compiler in the past seems to have carried out a peculiar arrangement of his own, many of them being rather difficult to comprehend. But of late a certain state of perfection has been attained by some of our best compilers, and their diction has been imitated by others, always, however, subject to some slight change to meet certain requirements that the work might present. The more clear and plain the style, the more readily it will be understood and appreciated. I prefer the method of arranging each generation in regular order by itself, and one generation after the other, with consecutive numbers prefixed and suffixed for reference, both forward and back, to the several names when they occur—as parent or child. The value of such records it is hardly possible to estimate, and the various connections and relationships that are developed by working out these family histories gives satisfaction to many a restless desire. In collecting material for the Rawson family memorial, persons were found who had lost all knowledge of some brother, uncle or cousin, who, through the working of some unforeseen change of events, had passed beyond reach of each other. In almost every instance, the persons themselves or their children were brought into communication with each other again.

If your patience will allow me, I would like to cite one instance which will perhaps better illustrate my meaning of the value to be placed on such pedigrees. . Some of you may recall an article that appeared in the Worcester *Daily Spy*, some months ago, relating to a Mr. Rawson, surgeon in the United States navy during the war of 1812. The close of that war found him in the port of Buenos Ayres, South America. He went into one of the interior provinces of what is now called the Argentine Republic, and settled in the city of Mendoza, capital of the province of Mendoza. Here he married a Spanish lady and became the father of two sons. In January, 1847, he died, after having devoted nearly thirty years of his life for the advancement of the best interests of the community where he lived and the education of his children. The eldest of them became an artist of some note in his own country, and died in 1871. The other son, Dr. Guillermo Rawson, now 55 years of age, is a graduate of both the University and Medical College of Buenos Ayres; was Minister Secretary of the Interior under General Mitre, receiving his appointment in 1862, and at present filling several posts of honor and trust, such as Senator in the Argentine Congress, Professor of Public Hygiene in the Medical Faculty of Buenos Ayres, Chairman of the Board of Consulting Physicians of the Sanitary Institute in that city, and also delegate to the International Medical Congress, which has just closed its session at Philadélphia. All the old family letters and papers belonging to the senior Dr. Rawson had been destroyed by fire before the sons were of sufficient age to remember their contents, and at their father's death all knowledge of their ancestry was lost; so that this educated, thinking man found himself without information concerning his progenitors beyond his own father, except he remembered that his father came from New England, and for the past ten or twelve years, through his own efforts as well as those of his friends, he had been trying to connect himself with some branch of the family here, but all to no purpose, and the matter had been dropped. But last Fall it was my privilege to find the connecting link, and I at once apprised him of the fact, at Buenos Ayres. The expression of joy and satisfaction that came in return from him in his letter to me, fully repaid me for the trouble I had taken in his behalf. This connection, doubtless, never would have been revealed had it not been for the republication of the Rawson memorial. It was the direct means of bringing about this happy result.

This centennial year will offer a rich harvest for the genealogist, as well as the historian. It has already awakened fresh interest in historical matters relating to our country, and genealogy must receive its share of attention.

A committee, consisting of Ellery B. Crane, Albert A. Lovell and Franklin P. Rice, was appointed to copy the inscriptions on the tombstones in Mechanic street and other old burial grounds in and about the city. At the meeting held November 11th, 1876, the above named committee made a partial report, stating that they have copied and arranged alphabetically more than 300 inscriptions, and that they propose to add short biographical sketches in a large number of cases. A final and complete report will not be made for some time to come.

At the close of 1876, we find that there is an increased interest being manifested on the part of our members and others in the advancement of the objects of the society, giving promise of a successful work in the years before us.

With abundant hope of future successes we finish the record of the year with a good measure of preparation for the labors and pleasures that await us.

PROCEEDINGS

FOR THE YEAR 1877.

The annual meeting was held at the residence of Samuel E. Staples, No. 1 Lincoln Place, Jan. 2d, 1877.

The revised Constitution, presented at the last regular meeting in 1876, was read by the Secretary and adopted.

The President then made a few congratulatory remarks relating to the progress of the Society during the past two years, stating that he deemed it unnecessary to make any formal address, as the entire ground would be covered by the annual reports of the several officers.

The Reports of the Secretary, Treasurer and Librarian were read and placed on file.

SECRETARY'S REPORT.

To the Officers and Members of The Worcester Society of Antiquity:

The Secretary, in reviewing the history and proceedings of the Society during the past two years, will not attempt any elaboration, but confine himself to a simple narration of facts, regretting that this duty should have fallen upon him for its performance, rather than upon another better qualified.

FIRST YEAR—1875.

The first preliminary meeting of this Society was held at the residence of Samuel E. Staples, No. 1 Lincoln Place, January 24, 1875, agreeably to an invitation given to several gentlemen to meet and consult upon the expediency of forming a society or association, the objects of which should be " to foster in its members a love and admiration for antiquarian research and archæological science, and to rescue from oblivion such historical matter as would otherwise be lost." There were present at this meeting Samuel E. Staples, John G. Smith, Franklin P. Rice and Richard O'Flynn. The subject of forming a society or association for such purposes was freely discussed, and the unanimously expressed opinion of those present was that such an organization would be useful and its mission beneficial, provided that a sufficient number of persons interested in its objects would unite in its formation, attend its meetings, and contribute to its interest and support. It was decided, before any formal action be taken, that another meeting be called and other persons of similar tastes be invited to be present. At this meeting Samuel E. Staples presented the draft of a Constitution—the substance of the present one—as a basis of the organization.

At the second preliminary meeting, held January 30, 1875, at the office of Tyler & Seagrave, No. 442 Main street, the meeting was organized by the choice of Samuel E. Staples as chairman, and Daniel Seagrave as secretary. There were present Samuel E. Staples, John G. Smith, Franklin P. Rice and Daniel Seagrave.

The subject of forming a society or association, as set forth in the letter of invitation, was considered, and it was unanimously voted to proceed with such purpose. The draft of a Constitution presented at the previous meeting was discussed at length, and subsequently referred to a committee, to report upon the same at a future meeting.

At the third preliminary meeting, held February 13, 1875, at the same place as the previous meeting, the committee to whom was referred the Constitution, made their report upon the same, which, with some slight amendments, was adopted.

At the first regular meeting, held March 2, 1875, at the office of Tyler & Seagrave, 442 Main street, the organization of the Society was completed by the election of the following officers :

SAMUEL E. STAPLES, *President.*
HENRY D. BARBER, *Vice President.*
DANIEL SEAGRAVE, *Secretary.*
HENRY F. STEDMAN, *Treasurer.*
JOHN G. SMITH, *Librarian.*

Reports of acquisitions by members to their respective collections have been made from time to time, showing what and how much each had gathered in his specialty.

The aggregate of collections during the first twelve months was quite satisfactory, possibly all that the most hopeful might have had reason to expect. Notwithstanding the paucity of our numbers, more than 1000 volumes and more than 1500 pamphlets, treating upon a great variety of subjects, besides much other valuable miscellaneous matter, such as portraits, views, autographs, coins, medals, etc., have been gathered, from which the history of the past may be written, and which shall be of advantage to the future historian. Among the many works collected are Belknap's History of New Hampshire, 3 vols.; Hutchinson's History of Massachusetts and Barber's Historical Collections; Williams' History of Vermont, 2 vols.; Whitney's History of Worcester County with map, published in 1793, and scores of town histories, historical addresses, etc., many of which are very valuable and hardly attainable at any price.

A good degree of interest has been manifested on the part of the members in their attendance at the meetings. At the close of the first year there were twelve names upon the roll of membership. Twelve meetings (three preliminary, nine regular and special,) have been held, in most cases at the residences of the members, by special invitation, and, although they have been somewhat informal and of a social character, yet they have been profitable and interesting.

SECOND YEAR—1876.

The second year of the existence of the Society has not been without its gratifying results—a growing interest, an increase of numbers, and a large average attendance at its meetings.

Two very interesting and instructive essays—one by Mr. Charles R. Johnson, upon the "Vestiges of Ancient American Civilization,"

and the other by Mr. Ellery B. Crane, the subject of which was
" Genealogy "—have been read before the Society during the past
year, and it is hoped that these may find a place in our Proceedings, whenever the same shall be published.

During the past year the Constitution has been carefully revised,
in order to meet the present and prospective wants of the Society.

I have the pleasure to report that the members have made large
and varied additions to their respective libraries and collections,
numbering in the aggregate nearly 1000 volumes of books, more
than 1500 pamphlets, 300 portraits and views, 700 coins and medals, and numerous autographs, etc. It is also gratifying to know
that much of this valuable historical matter—much of it gathered
from the waste-box, and thus snatched from the jaws of the paper
mill—is saved to enrich the literary resources of the city of Worcester.

Among the many rare and valuable volumes secured and deserving mention in this report, many of which are fine specimens of
printing and well preserved, are the following :

Piers' Ploughman (written,)---------------------------1302
Sermones Quadragisimales, Utino, (illum.) Venice ------1473
Svetonivs De Vita XII. Cæsarvm,------- Milan----------1475
De Preceptis (illuminated,)-------------Venice-------..1478
New Testament (reprint,)---------- -----Cologne-------.1526
New Testament (reprint,)----------------Geneva--------1557
Daynty Deuises,------------------------London--------1576
Breeches Bible (illustrated,)------------London--------1616
Mappe of Rome,---- --------------------London--------1620
David's Teares,------------------------London--------1632
Quarles' Emblems (illustrated,)----------London--------1634
Overbury's Wife,-----------------------London--------1638
Ovid's Metamorphoses,------------------London--------1640
Critica Sacra,-------------------------London--------1642
Lof Sanck,--------------------------Amsterdam----1650
Gondibert,------ ------ ---------------London--------1651
Middle State of Souls,------------------London--------1659
Field's Bible, 2 vols., folio (illustrated,)---Cambridge.. ..1660
Muggleton's Works,--------------------London--------1661
Works of Jacob Cats (illustrated,)-------Amsterdam----1665
Theatre of Human Life (illustrated,)-----Brussels-------1672
Clavis Homericus,---------------------Rotterdam-----1673
Baxter's Saint's Rest,------------------London--------1688
Meditations of Antoninus,--------------London--------1692

THE OLDEST BOOK IN WORCESTER COUNTY.—" *Sermones
Quadragisimales de legibus fratris Leonardi De Utino sacre theo-
logie doctoris.*" This is the title of a large folio volume, containing 800 pages, in Latin, printed on thick paper, without
title page or date, as was the case with the first books printed.
Upon the back of the cover, which is of wood and covered with
hog skin, is the date 1473–5, but it is the opinion of good
judges that it is even older than those figures indicate. The leaves
are without running title, number of pages, signatures, or divisions
into paragraphs. It is printed in ancient black letter, and the
words at the ends of lines are not divided by hyphens. It has
two columns on each page, with wide margin, and the words are
very much abbreviated, with no punctuation marks except the
colon and period. Proper names and sentences are begun with
small letters, and the name and residence of the printer, as well as
the date, were omitted, all of which indicate great antiquity. This
book is illuminated from beginning to end, on every page, and is
probably the best preserved book of its age in this country.

Since the above was written, it has been ascertained from a
work in the American Antiquarian Society's Library that this
book was printed at Venice in 1473.

Another Rarity.—I must not fail to mention an edition of "*Sretonirs De Vita XII. Carsarrm, Mediolani*, 1475," (Suetonius' Lives of the Twelve Cæsars, published in Milan in 1475.) A brief description I quote somewhat from the language of another.

This work was executed by Philip de Lauagnia, who styled himself the first printer of the Latin race, and was associated for a time with Antonius Zarotus, afterwards with the German Waldopel, and later with John Bonus. This book, which is a fine specimen of early printing, and in excellent preservation, is printed on heavy paper sized with parchment, a greater portion of the pages being as bright and clean as when they left the press, while on others are annotations in Latin. Space is left throughout the work for illuminated initials to be inserted by hand, which work was never done. It is a quarto, with wide margin, and compares remarkably well with the best specimens of modern printing. From a manuscript note on the fly leaf, the book is supposed to have once belonged to the library of Lord Spencer.

Books published at so early a date are exceedingly rare, it being but about thirty-five years after the first use of metal type with engraved faces. The publication of the Lives of the Cæsars precedes by one year the first Greek book ever printed, which was the Greek Grammar of Constantine Lascaris, executed at Milan by Dionysius Paravisinus, in 1476, and by six years the first printed portion of the Holy Scriptures in Greek—viz.: The Psalms—issued there in 1481. There is in the Library of the Athenæum at Turin a book printed by Philip de Lauagnia in Milan, bearing date of 1469, viz.: "The Miracles of Notre Dame." The oldest printed volume in possession of the American Antiquarian Society, located in this city, is a Latin translation of Herodotus, printed by Arnold Pennartz, at Rome, in 1475.

Among the rarest of American publications may be mentioned the following original edition: "A Modest Inquiry into the Nature of Witchcraft, and How Persons Guilty of that Crime may be Convicted: And the Means used for their Discovery Discussed, both Negatively and Affirmatively, according to Scripture and Experience. By John Hale, Pastor of the Church of Christ in Beverly. With an Introduction to the work, by John Higginson,

Pastor of the Church in Salem. Anno Domini 1697. *Boston in N. E. Printed by B. Green, and F. Allen, for Benjamin Eliot.*" In the catalogue of Mr. William Menzies' collection this work is classed as EXCESSIVELY RARE, indeed the rarest of all the works relating to the New England Witchcraft Delusion. So far as known, there are but *three* copies of this work extant.

In connection with Eliot's Indian Bible, for rarity, may be mentioned the following work, only *five* copies of which are now known to exist, and are to be found in the libraries of the American Antiquarian Society, the Massachusetts Historical Society, the Prince Library, the collection of the late George Brinley, and in the private collection of Mr. John G. Smith, the Librarian of this Society. This work is printed in English on one page, and on the opposite page in the Indian or Algonkin language, which was the spoken language of the aborigines of New England. It is dedicated " To the Honorable William Stoughton, Esq., Lieutenant GOVERNOUR of His Majestie's Province of the Massachusetts Bay in New England; and to the Reverend Increase Mather, D. D., Teacher of the Second Church of Christ in Boston, and President of Harvard College in Cambridge." The title is as follows: "A CONFESSION OF FAITH Owned & consented unto by the Elders & Messengers of the Churches Assembled at *Boston* in *New England*, May 12. 1680. Being the Second Session of that SYNOD.—Eph. 4. 5 [and Col. 2. 5; 3 lines].—BOSTON. Re-printed by *Bartholomew Green*, and *John Allen.* 1699."

The Indian title page reads as follows:

" Wunnamptamoe SAMPOOAONK Wussampoowontamun Nashpe mocuwchkomunganash ut *New-England*. Qushkenumun en *Indiane* Unnontowaonganit.—Nashpe *Grindal Rawson, &c.* . . . . MUSHAUWOMUK. Printeuun nashpe *Bartholomew Green*, kah *John Allen.* 1699. 16mo."

Another work of more than ordinary interest is entitled : " Indian Converts: or Some Account of the Lives and Dying Speeches of a Considerable Number of the Christianized Indians of Martha's Vineyard, in New England, viz.: I. Of Godly Ministers. II. Of Other Good Men. III. Of Religious Women. IV. Of Pious

Young Persons. By Experience Mayhew, M. A., Preacher of the Gospel to the Indians of that Island. To which is added, Some Account of those English Ministers who have Successively Presided over the Indian work in that and the adjacent Islands. By Mr. Prince. 8", pp. xxiv., 310, 16. *London: Printed for Samuel Gerrish, in New England. 1727.*"

Such a collection of rarities as the above ought not to be scattered, but, on the other hand, saved complete, to increase the literary wealth of some public institution in our city or county.

The meetings of the Society during the past year have been held as formerly, at the residences of its members. While all have been pleasantly accommodated, and each and all cordially welcomed thereto, wherever the meeting has been held, yet all have felt the need, as our numbers increased, of larger accommodations at some central point, easily accessible to all. It is hoped that the time is not far in the future when the members shall realize all that they have ever anticipated—in having a pleasant and commodious place for holding their meetings, and a good library, with its useful appendages, etc., for their convenience and enjoyment.

The Society has held twelve meetings during the past year, with a fair average attendance of its members at each session.

At this date the Society has a membership of thirty—twenty-seven active and three honorary members.

Respectfully submitted.

DANIEL SEAGRAVE, *Secretary.*

Worcester, Mass., Jan. 2, 1877.

The meetings of the Society, thus far, having been held at the residences of the members, and the few expenses incurred having been paid by voluntary contributions, up to January 1st, 1877, the duties of the Treasurer have been far from burdensome, as will be seen by the following report:

7

· TREASURER'S REPORT.

WORCESTER, MASS., Jan. 2, 1877.

JAMES A. SMITH, *Treasurer pro tem., in account with*
THE WORCESTER SOCIETY OF ANTIQUITY.

1876. *Dr.*		*Cr.*	
Cash received of Secretary, Daniel Seagrave	$4 00	Cash paid to Tyler & Seagrave	$4 00
Cash received of President, Samuel E. Staples	1 00	Cash on hand	1 00
	$5 00		$5 00

JAMES A. SMITH, *Treasurer pro tem.*

LIBRARIAN'S REPORT.

It is unnecessary to say that this Society was formed for the purpose of collecting books and other historical matter, without the expectation of establishing a library for public consultation, though it was supposed by some that such might be the result at some future day.

During the first year of our existence as a Society, each member made collections for himself, without much reference to the fact that a large portion of the libraries of the several members might be brought together as one; but during the present year such interest has been manifested in our efforts as to warrant the hope that this Society may soon establish a library for public use.

We have received the following donations:

ALBERT A. LOVELL.—His "Worcester in the War of the Revolution; Embracing the Acts of the Town of Worcester from 1765 to 1783, inclusive, with an Appendix."

ELLERY B. CRANE.—His "Rawson Family.—A Revised Memoir of Edward Rawson, Secretary of the Colony of Massachusetts Bay from 1650 to 1686, with Genealogical Notes of his Descendants."

HON. CHARLES HUDSON.—The Dedication of Town and Memorial Hall, Lexington, 1871;" his "Abstract of the History of Lexington, from its First Settlement to the Centennial Anniversary of the Declaration of our National Independence, July 4th, 1876;" his "Lexington Centennial, 1775 to 1785."

DANIEL SEAGRAVE.—Three Centennial Exhibition pamphlets.

RICHARD O'FLYNN.—Psalm Book and Record Book.

NATHANIEL PAINE (for the City Committee on Printing the Fourth of July Proceedings.)—"Celebration by the Inhabitants of Worcester, Mass., of the Centennial Anniversary of the Declaration of Independence, July 4th, 1876."

CLARK JILLSON.—"Celebration by the Inhabitants of Worcester, Mass., of the Centennial Anniversary of the Declaration of Independence, July 4th, 1876, including the Oration of Hon. Benjamin F. Thomas, LL.D., to which are added Historical and Chronological Notes;" "Singing by the Pupils of the Public Schools, July 4th, 1876;" his "Address Delivered at Worcester, Feb. 10th, 1874, at the First Reunion of the Sons of Vermont; together with Toasts, Sentiments, Speeches, Poetry and Song;" his "Valedictory Address, delivered before the City Council of Worcester, December 29th, 1876."

Respectfully submitted,

JOHN G. SMITH, Librarian.

Worcester, Mass., Jan. 2, 1877.

The Society then proceeded to elect its officers, as follows:

President—SAMUEL E. STAPLES.
Vice Presidents—ELLERY B. CRANE, CLARK JILLSON.
Secretary—DANIEL SEAGRAVE.
Treasurer—JAMES A. SMITH.
Librarian—JOHN G. SMITH.

EXECUTIVE COMMITTEE.

SAMUEL E. STAPLES, | ELLERY B. CRANE,
CLARK JILLSON, | DANIEL SEAGRAVE,
JAMES A. SMITH.

STANDING COMMITTEE ON NOMINATIONS.

ALBERT A. LOVELL, for one year.
FRANKLIN P. RICE, for two years.
CHARLES R. JOHNSON, for three years.

Clark Jillson was appointed a committee of one to take such action as might be necessary to incorporate the Society under the laws of the Commonwealth, and the Secretary was appointed a committee to prepare a design for a seal.

The Committee on the "Old Burial Grounds" made a partial report in relation to biographical sketches of some of those interred therein, several of which were read by Albert A. Lovell, to the great satisfaction of all present.

The Society then adjourned to meet on the third Tuesday evening of January, 1877, at the residence of Ellery B. Crane, No. 19 Benefit street.

The adjourned annual meeting was held as per adjournment, and the Executive Committee, to whom was referred the matter of the publication of the transactions of the Society had been referred, made the following report, which was adopted :

REPORT.

To the President of The Worcester Society of Antiquity :

The Executive Committee, to whom was referred the matter of printing the Proceedings of THE WORCESTER SOCIETY OF ANTIQUITY, have attended to the business submitted to them, and report :

That the interests of the Society at the present time seem to require the publication of its Proceedings for the years 1875–'6. Your committee deem it of great importance that this publication should embrace a minute, detailed account of the organization of the Society, giving such facts and dates as may be useful for future reference ; and they appointed Clark Jillson, one of their number, to prepare the matter for publication, all of which is now nearly completed.

For the purpose of defraying the expense of this publication, we recommend the levy of an assessment upon the active members of the Society of three dollars each ; and that each member paying such assessment be entitled to two copies, with the right to purchase others at such price as the Society may determine.

All of which is respectfully submitted.

SAMUEL E. STAPLES,
CLARK JILLSON,
ELLERY B. CRANE,
DANIEL SEAGRAVE,
JAMES A. SMITH.

The committee, Daniel Seagrave, who was appointed for the purpose, presented a design for a Seal, and upon his suggestion it was voted that each member of the Society be invited to prepare a design and present the same for inspection at the next meeting.

The Society voted to levy an assessment upon the members of three dollars each to defray the expense of printing the Proceedings, as recommended by the Executive Committee, and the meeting was then adjourned.

The following letters have been received from those who have been elected honorary members of this Society:

————

CAMBRIDGEPORT, Mass., Nov. 27, 1876.

DEAR SIR—Yours of the 24th instant, announcing my election as an honorary member of THE WORCESTER SOCIETY OF ANTIQUITY is at hand. I pray you to assure the Society that I fully appreciate the honor thus conferred upon me.

Truly yours,
LUCIUS R. PAIGE.

DANIEL SEAGRAVE, Esq., Secretary, etc.

————

LEXINGTON, Dec. 30, 1876.

To Daniel Seagrave, Esq., Secretary of Wor. Society of Antiquity:

DEAR SIR:—Your favor of the 16th, informing me that I have been elected an honorary member of THE WORCESTER SOCIETY OF

ANTIQUITY, was duly received. I hereby signify my acceptance of the position, and my thanks for the honor conferred upon me. If I can aid you in your object, I shall gladly do it. · I send you herewith a small packet of pamphlets.

Respectfully yours,
CHARLES HUDSON.

WORCESTER, Mass., Feb. 13, 1877.

Daniel Seagrave, Esq., Secretary of
The Worcester Society of Antiquity:

DEAR SIR—I have received your communication informing me that I have been "unanimously elected an honorary member" of your Society. Allow me, through you, to express my thanks to the Society for this honor and expression of good will. I have full sympathy with the aims of your Society, and I shall find special pleasure in doing what I can to aid it in promoting these aims. I should rejoice to see the disposition to "remember the days that are past," and to collect, for preservation, memorials of the past generations, much more prevalent than it is now.

Very respectfully, yours,
JOHN D. BALDWIN.

Mr. Daniel Seagrave, Secretary,

DEAR SIR:—I am in receipt of your notice that I have been chosen an Honorary Member of "The Worcester Society of Antiquity." With my acceptance of the honor, I desire to express to you and your associates my thanks, and my appreciation of your kindness.

Very truly, your friend,
CLARENDON HARRIS.

WORCESTER, Feb'y 17, 1877.

At the regular meeting held February 6th, at the residence of James A Smith, No. 31 Wachusett street, several designs for a Seal were presented and

examined. The Secretary was instructed to invite
all the members of the Society to prepare and bring
designs to his office and express their preference
after careful examination of all those presented. The
President and Vice-Presidents were appointed a Committee to select a design for a Seal from those to be
presented, or make such combination of any two or
more as they might think best, and cause a Seal to
be engraved therefrom.

Mr. Thomas J. Hastings, Representative to the
General Court from Dist. No. 18, presented the Society with ten volumes of public documents.

At the meeting held March 6th, 1877, at the residence of Edward I. Comins, No. 46 Wellington street,
a communication was received and read by the Secretary from Clarendon Harris, Esq., of Worcester, in
acknowledgment of his election to Honorary Membership in this Society.

Mr. Jillson, at the request of the Chairman of the
Committee on procuring a Seal, read the following
report which was accepted, and the Seal which the
Committee had procured was adopted as the Seal of
the Society.

REPORT.

The Committee appointed to select a design and procure a Seal
for The Worcester Society of Antiquity, have attended to the
duty assigned them and submit the following Report:

At the annual meeting of the Society, held January 2d, Daniel
Seagrave was appointed a Committee to prepare a design for a
Seal, and in the performance of that duty, he presented one for
inspection at the adjourned meeting held January 16th. At this
meeting, upon his request, it was voted that the other members of

the Society be requested to prepare and present designs at the following meeting. Ellery B. Crane, Dwight A. Davis, Albert Tyler, and Daniel Seagrave, responded to the invitation.

Subsquently, in accordance with a vote of the Society, requesting all the members to prepare and bring in designs for examination at the office of the Secretary, E. R. Lawrence, E. H. Marshall, John G. Smith, and Henry Phelps, complied with the request, which, together with those before presented, made a total number of twelve. Either one of these was well conceived, truly suggestive, and in some respects, well adapted to the purpose proposed. But as there were various designs, so as a matter of course, there was a difference of opinion as to which design was best suited to our purpose. It was therefore voted, that the whole matter be referred to a Committee consisting of Samuel E. Staples, Clark Jillson, and Ellery B. Crane, with authority to make a selection and procure the engraving of a Seal, after the members should have an opportunity to pass judgment upon the designs presented and express their choice in the matter. This opportunity was given them on February 10th, at the office of the Secretary, when the last designs were presented in accordance with the vote of the Society.

The Committee in the performance of the duty assigned them, after a careful consideration of the various designs presented, and in accordance with the suggestion of a number of members of the Society, thought it best to make a combination of ideas contained in a number of the designs, thus securing a more perfect embodiment of thought than was manifest in any one of those submitted to them.

The Society has a very wide and extensive range for its inquiries and researches, as its name indicates, and in this may be seen the fitness of the emblems adopted. The Committee will not attempt to give a full description of the Seal which they present as the result of their labors, but will only explain a few of the leading thoughts which they think it aptly presents to the consideration of the intelligent student of history. The prominent figure in the foreground and that which first attracts the attention, is a representation of a vase found in one of the mounds of the State of Ohio. This indicates earlier civilizations and settlements of this

57

Continent than till within a few years, had been supposed probable. But late researches have established the fact beyond a reasonable doubt, of a settlement here, and an advanced state of civilization, that was not known by the early writers and historians of this land. Ancient implements of war are also grouped together, and beneath them all are the volumes of archeological science exemplifying the legend upon the scroll, " *Litera scripta manet*."— " the written letter remains." The distant perspective presents the Pyramids, the Sphinx, and Cleopatra's Needle, all indicating the early civilization of Egypt, the seat of ancient learning.

The Committee would have been glad to have incorporated with these emblems something especially suggestive of New England history, but it was found difficult to select a suitable emblem that has not already been used by some other kindred Society.

We would hereby express our thanks to each and all of the gentlemen who have in any way assisted us in this matter, and submit as the result of our completed, though somewhat difficult task, the accompanying Seal, which we hope may be acceptable to all who are now or may hereafter become members of THE WORCESTER SOCIETY OF ANTIQUITY.

Respectfully submitted,

SAMUEL E. STAPLES.
CLARK JILLSON.
ELLERY B. CRANE.

Worcester, March 6, 1877.

The Committee appointed January 2d, to take action in relation to procuring an Act of Incorporation, made the following report, which was accepted, and its recommendations adopted:

To the President and Members of The Worcester Society of Antiquity:

The Committee to whom was referred the matter of taking measures to obtain an Act of Incorporation, report:—

That the Society may become a corporate body under the General Laws of the Commonwealth; and that an agreement has

8

been duly signed by the requisite number of persons, members of this Society, who have been legally notified to meet here at this time, for the purpose of organizing a corporation, to be known by the name of THE WORCESTER SOCIETY OF ANTIQUITY.

Your Committee recommend that those persons who have been thus legally notified, proceed at once to organize a corporation as and for the purposes set forth in said agreement, in accordance with the Laws of the Commonwealth.

Respectfully submitted,

CLARK JILLSON,

Committee.

Worcester, March 6, 1877.

The above report was accepted, and its recommendations adopted.

The meeting was then adjourned *sine die.*

DANIEL SEAGRAVE,

Secretary.

INCORPORATION

— of —

The Worcester Society of Antiquity.

AGREEMENT.

We, whose names are hereto subscribed, do, by this agreement, associate ourselves with the intention to constitute a corporation according to the provisions of the three hundred and seventy-fifth chapter of the Acts of the General Court of the Commonwealth of Massachusetts, passed in the year eighteen hundred and seventy-four, approved June twenty-seventh, in said year.

The name by which the corporation shall be known is The Worcester Society of Antiquity.

The purpose for which the corporation is constituted is: —

1st. To cultivate and encourage among its members a love and admiration for antiquarian research and archæological science; and, so far as possible, to rescue from oblivion any historical matter that might otherwise be lost.

2d. The collection and preservation of antiquarian relics of every description.

The place within which the corporation is established or located is the city of Worcester, within said Commonwealth.

In witness whereof, we have hereunto set our hands, this twentieth day of February, in the year eighteen hundred and seventy-seven.

Samuel Elias Staples,
Clark Jillson,
Ellery Bicknell Crane,
Daniel Seagrave,
Richard O'Flynn,

Franklin Pierce Rice,
Albert Tyler,
James A. Smith,
Albert Alfonzo Lovell.

One of the subscribers to the above agreement notified said subscribers of the first meeting, by giving each in hand a true and attested copy of the following notice, as herein set forth :

You are hereby notified, that the first meeting of the subscribers to an agreement to associate themselves with the intention to constitute a corporation to be known by the name of THE WORCESTER SOCIETY OF ANTIQUITY, dated February 20th, 1877, for the purpose of organizing said corporation by the adoption of By-Laws and election of officers, and the transaction of such other business as may properly come before the meeting, will be held on Tuesday, the sixth day of March, 1877, at half-past seven o'clock P. M., at the residence of Edward I. Comins, No. 46 Wellington street.

DANIEL SEAGRAVE,
One of the subscribers to said agreement.

WORCESTER, Mass., Feb. 20, 1877.

———

Commonwealth of Massachusetts.

WORCESTER, ss.

I, Daniel Seagrave, do hereby certify, that on the twentieth day of February, A. D., 1877, I duly served the within notice upon Samuel Elias Staples, Clark Jillson, Ellery Bicknell Crane, Richard O'Flynn, Franklin Pierce Rice, Albert Tyler, James A. Smith and Albert Alfonzo Lovell, they being subscribers to an agreement to associate themselves with the intention to constitute a corporation, to be known by the name of THE WORCESTER SOCIETY OF ANTIQUITY, by giving in hand to each of said subscribers a true and attested copy thereof.

DANIEL SEAGRAVE,
One of the subscribers to said agreement.

———

WORCESTER, ss.

Subscribed and sworn to this twenty-seventh day of February, A. D., 1877, before me.

CLARK JILLSON,
Justice of the Peace.

The first meeting held in conformity with the foregoing notice, was called to order by Clark Jillson, and Daniel Seagrave was elected temporary Clerk, by ballot, and was sworn to the faithful discharge of his duty.

Commonwealth of Massachusetts.

WORCESTER, ss.   March 6th, 1877.

Then personally appeared the above-named Daniel Seagrave, and made oath that he would faithfully perform the duties of temporary Clerk of The Worcester Society of Antiquity.

Before me,

CLARK JILLSON,
Justice of the Peace.

The subscribers then proceeded to elect, by ballot: Daniel Seagrave, Clerk; Samuel Elias Staples, President; Clark Jillson and Ellery B. Crane, Vice-Presidents; James A. Smith, Treasurer; Samuel E. Staples, Clark Jillson, Ellery B. Crane, Daniel Seagrave and James A. Smith, Executive Committee.

The Clerk and Treasurer, upon their election, were duly sworn, as follows:

Commonwealth of Massachusetts.

WORCESTER, ss.   March 6th, 1877.

Then personally appeared the above-named Daniel Seagrave, Clerk, and James Andrew Smith, Treasurer, of The Worcester Society of Antiquity, and made oath that they would faithfully perform the duties of their respective offices.

Before me,

CLARK JILLSON,
Justice of the Peace.

The members of The Worcester Society of Anti-quity, viz. : John George Smith, Henry Davis Barber, Henry Francis Stedman, William Macready, Olin L. Merriam, Herbert H. Thompson, Elijah H. Marshall, William A. Sheldon, William B. Howe, Charles R. Johnson, Augustus Stone, Edwin R. Lawrence, Henry Phelps, Augustus Cooledge, Thomas E. St. John, Edward I. Comins, Thomas M. Lamb, Dwight A. Davis and Benjamin J. Dodge ; together with Isaac N. Metcalf, George Sumner, Joseph N. Bates, Alexander C. Munroe and Charles W. Estabrook, were constituted members of the corporation.

The Constitution and By-Laws of The Worcester Society of Antiquity were adopted as the By-Laws of the corporation.

John G. Smith was elected, by ballot, as Librarian.

The following members were elected the Standing Committee on Nominations :

Albert A. Lovell, to serve one year ; Franklin P. Rice, to serve two years ; and Charles R. Johnson, to serve three years.

The President, Clerk, Treasurer, and a majority of the Executive Committee, then made, signed, and made oath to the following certificate :

We, Samuel Elias Staples, President; James Andrew Smith, Treasurer ; Daniel Seagrave, Clerk, Ellery B. Crane, and Clark Jillson, the same being a majority of the Executive Committee of The Worcester Society of Antiquity, in compliance with the requirements of the fourth section of chapter three hundred and seventy-five of the Acts of the year eighteen hundred and seventy-four, do hereby certify that the following is a true copy of the agreement of association to constitute said corporation, with the names of the subscribers thereto :

" We, whose names are hereto subscribed, do, by this agreement, associate ourselves with the intention to constitute a corporation according to the provisions of the three hundred and seventy-fifth chapter of the Acts of the General Court of the Commonwealth of Massachusetts, passed in the year eighteen hundred and seventy-four, approved June twenty-seventh in said year. The name by which the corporation shall be known, is THE WORCESTER SOCIETY OF ANTIQUITY.

The purpose for which the corporation is constituted is,—

1st. To cultivate and encourage among its members a love and admiration for antiquarian research and archæological science, and, so far as possible, to rescue from oblivion, any historical matter that might otherwise be lost.

2nd. The collection and preservation of antiquarian relics of every description.

The place within which the corporation is established or located, is the city of Worcester, within said Commonwealth.

In witness whereof, we have hereunto set our hands, this twentieth day of February, in the year eighteen hundred and seventy-seven.

SAMUEL ELIAS STAPLES, JAMES ANDREW SMITH,
CLARK JILLSON, ALBERT ALFONZO LOVELL,
ELLERY B. CRANE, RICHARD O'FLYNN,
DANIEL SEAGRAVE, ALBERT TYLER."
FRANKLIN PIERCE RICE,

That the first meeting of the subscribers to said agreement was held on the sixth day of March, in the year eighteen hundred and seventy-seven.

In witness whereof, we have hereunto signed our names, this sixth day of March, in the year eighteen hundred and seventy-seven.

SAMUEL ELIAS STAPLES, DANIEL SEAGRAVE,
CLARK JILLSON, JAMES ANDREW SMITH.
ELLERY B. CRANE,

A majority of the Executive Committee of THE WORCESTER SOCIETY OF ANTIQUITY.

64

Commonwealth of Massachusetts.

WORCESTER, ss.   March 6th, 1877.

Then personally appeared the above-named Samuel Elias Staples, Ellery B. Crane, Daniel Seagrave, and James Andrew Smith, being a majority of the Executive Committtee of THE WORCESTER SOCIETY OF ANTIQUITY, and severally made oath that the foregoing certificate, by them subscribed, is true to the best of their knowledge and belief.

Before me,

CLARK JILLSON,
Justice of the Peace.

_____

The Society then voted that the imprint hereto affixed be, and the same is hereby established as the seal of this Society.

The following named gentlemen were elected Honorary Members of this Society, viz.:   Rev. Lucius R. Paige, D. D., of Cambridgeport ; Clarendon Harris, Esq., of Worcester ; Hon. Charles Hudson, of Lexington ; and Hon. John Dennison Baldwin, A. M., of Worcester.

DANIEL SEAGRAVE, Clerk.

A true copy.

Attest: DANIEL SEAGRAVE, Clerk.

CONSTITUTION.

ARTICLE I.

NAME.

This Society shall be called THE WORCESTER SOCIETY OF ANTIQUITY.

ARTICLE II.

OBJECT.

The purposes of this Society shall be:

1. To cultivate and encourage among its members a love and admiration for antiquarian research and archæological science; and, so far as possible, to rescue from oblivion any historical matter that might otherwise be lost.

2. The collection and preservation of antique relics of every description.

ARTICLE III.

OFFICERS.

The officers of this Society shall consist of a President, two Vice Presidents, Secretary, Treasurer and Librarian. Each officer shall be elected by ballot, and only one officer shall be balloted for at the same time. A majority of the ballots shall be sufficient to elect. They shall hold office for the term of one year, and until their successors are chosen.

ARTICLE IV.

DUTIES OF OFFICERS.

1. *President.* It shall be the duty of the President to preside at all meetings, when present. In his absence the First Vice President shall preside; in the absence of the latter, the Second Vice President shall preside; and in the absence of all three, a President *pro tem.* shall be chosen.

2. *Secretary.* It shall be the duty of the Secretary to keep a record of all meetings of the Society in a book provided for that purpose; to issue all notices of meetings, with the time and place of same; to conduct the general correspondence of the Society; shall notify all persons of their election as members of the Society; shall notify all members elected to office, who were not present at the time of their election, within ten days thereafter; and at the expiration of his term of office shall turn over to his successor all books and papers in his possession belonging to the Society.

3. *Treasurer.* The Treasurer shall be sole custodian of the funds of the Society, and of all property, or titles to property, real or personal, belonging to the Society, except its books. He shall assess and collect all dues and taxes voted by the Society, receive any legacies bequeathed or donations made to its funds; shall disburse the moneys so received and collected, on a written order signed by the President and Secretary, but not otherwise. He shall keep in a book provided for the purpose a true account of all receipts and disbursements; shall submit the same to the inspection of any member, when the request is made; shall submit in writing a report of all his receipts and disbursements for the year, and exhibit his vouchers for same at each annual meeting; shall furnish a bond for the faithful discharge of his duties, whenever the Society, by a vote, may so direct; and shall, at the expiration of his term of office, place in the hands of his successor all books papers and other property in his possession belonging to the Society.

4. *Librarian.* The Librarian shall be the sole custodian of books and pamphlets belonging to the Society; shall catalogue the same in a book kept for the purpose; shall have the care of the entire collection of relics belonging to the Society, together with the room in which they are kept, and shall report the condition of same at each annual meeting.

ARTICLE V.
COMMITTEES.

1. The President, First and Second Vice Presidents, Secretary and Treasurer shall constitute a committee of five, to be known as the Executive Committee, who shall have in charge the general

interest of the Society; shall prepare for press and have the care of all publications of the Society, unless by a vote the Society see fit, when desirable, to elect a special committee for that purpose; may prepare and present business; may solicit and secure, when practicable, donations to the Society's funds, or collections; shall see that the orders of the Society are promptly carried out, and that the provisions of this Constitution are studiously maintained. The President *ex-officio* shall at each annual meeting make a report of the proceedings of the Society for the previous year.

2. This Society shall, at its annual meeting in January, 1877, elect by ballot three persons—one to serve for one year, one for two years, and one for three years—and one for three years at each annual meeting succeeding—who shall be called the Standing Committee on Nominations. It shall be their duty to examine the qualifications of every person proposed for membership, and to put in nomination such persons as they in their judgment think will promote the interests of the Society. Other committees may be chosen, as occasion requires, but all committees shall report their doings in writing.

ARTICLE VI.
MEMBERS.

1. The name and qualifications for membership of any person of good character, having an interest in the objects of this Society, may be proposed at any meeting thereof and referred to the Standing Committee on Nominations; and such person may, at the next regular meeting, on nomination by the said committee, be elected by a two-thirds ballot of those present. But no person shall be considered a member of this Society until he has signed the Constitution.

ARTICLE VII.
HONORARY.

Honorary members may be proposed and elected in the same manner as prescribed for active members.

ARTICLE VIII.
DUTIES OF MEMBERS.

1. It shall be the duty of each member to bear his equal burden of the expense of the Society, and to fill any office or perform any

service to which he may be elected or appointed; to endeavor to secure for it whatever he can that will add to the number or value of the Society's collection; to bring it to the knowledge and consideration of persons of similar tastes and pursuits; to propose for membership such persons as are known to be interested in its work.

2. It shall be the duty of honorary members to endeavor to secure articles for its collection, to interest themselves for its honor and prosperity, and to correspond at least once a year with the Society. They shall be entitled to all the privileges of active members, except the right to vote or hold office.

ARTICLE IX.
MEETINGS.

The annual meeting for the election of officers, and for the transaction of other business, shall be held on the first Tuesday in January of each year. The other regular meetings shall be held on the first Tuesday of each of the remaining months in the year, excepting July and August. Special meetings may be called by the President, or upon the written request of any three members of the Society. *Five* members shall constitute a quorum for the transaction of business.

ARTICLE X.
ASSESSMENTS AND DISBURSEMENTS.

I. *Tax.* The Society may at any regular meeting, by a vote, assess a tax upon its members, not exceeding one dollar *per capita*; but at any annual meeting the Society may assess such sum as may be needed for carrying on the affairs of the Society.

2. *Life Membership.* Any member who shall at any one time pay into the treasury the sum of twenty-five dollars shall be a life member, and shall thereafter be exempt from all assessments.

3. *Claims against.* All claims against the Society shall be approved by the member contracting the same, and paid by the Treasurer, on a written order signed by the President and Secretary.

69

ARTICLE XI.

FAILURES, WITHDRAWALS, EXPULSIONS.

1. Any member who for two consecutive years shall fail to pay any assessment made in accordance with the provisions of this Constitution, and shall give no satisfactory reason therefor, shall cease to be a member of the Society, and the Treasurer shall notify the Secretary, who shall make record of the fact.

2. *Withdrawals.* Any member may withdraw from the Society by giving notice of his intention to the Secretary and paying all assessments due at the time of giving such notice, and the Secretary shall make record of the fact.

3. *Expulsions.* Any member may, from any breach of trust or malfeasance in office, or for any other cause, be expelled from the Society by a vote of two-thirds of those present at any regular meeting; *provided*, that the number present shall not be less than a majority of the whole number of members. But no member shall be expelled from the Society without first having an opportunity to explain his case at some regular meeting.

ARTICLE XII.

AMENDMENTS.

Alterations or amendments to the Constitution may be made at any regular meeting, by a two-thirds vote; *provided*, that a notice of the proposed change has been given in writing at some previous meeting.

ARTICLE XIII.

On the passage and adoption of the foregoing Constitution, all other articles previously used for the government of this Society are hereby repealed.